About the Author

Peter Denison was commissioned from the RMA, Sandhurst, into an infantry regiment. He resigned his commission in the rank of Captain in order to commence training as a probation officer, remaining in the Probation Service for thirty-seven years. After becoming a Christian in 1974, he was involved in various Christian rehabilitation offender related charities, including Probation Service Christian Fellowship (National Chairman), Prison Fellowship (South East England Coordinator) and Stepping Stones Trust (SST Chairman for twenty-eight years), receiving an OBE for his work in SST. He has a passionate interest in seeing the Lord working in the lives of prisoners.

The Truth Will Set You Free

Peter Denison

The Truth Will Set You Free

Olympia Publishers
London

www.olympiapublishers.com
OLYMPIA PAPERBACK EDITION

A CIP catalogue record for this title is
available from the British Library.

ISBN: 978-1-80439-011-5

First Published in 2023

Olympia Publishers
Tallis House
2 Tallis Street
London
EC4Y 0AB

Printed in Great Britain

Dedication

I dedicate this book to the Lord Jesus Christ, who inspired me to write it.

Contents

Part 1
Seekers.

Following my two books on prison ministry, this third book addresses various Christian topics, some quite controversial. It is written for Christians and those interested in exploring Christianity, whom I have called 'seekers'.

1.
The Truth, Accuracy and Reliability of the Bible

Almost everything that I have had published refers to passages from the Bible. Therefore, the purpose of this first chapter is to ascertain the truth, accuracy and reliability of the Bible. Those unsure about Christianity sometimes use the following argument to justify their position: "I reject all you say about Christianity because I don't believe in the Bible." This is a reasonable viewpoint, provided it is reached after considering the evidence that supports Biblical accuracy, some of which I will explore in this article.

God is particularly keen on seeing faith in humanity, so is reluctant to make His presence too obvious, as this may reduce the need for faith. Nevertheless, there are times when God does allow factual evidence to be revealed in support of the Bible's account of the history of humanity.

One such example is the discovery of Noah's Ark in 1959 by a Turkish army captain called Durupinar, who noticed from an aerial reconnaissance photo of a Turkish mountain that there was the shape of a large boat. When subsequently investigated, it was confirmed that this man-made structure was the exact length (515 feet or 300 Royal Egyptian Cubits), and in the location, of the ark described in the Bible (Genesis 8:4), *'The ark came to rest on the mountains of Ararat.'* Ararat is the name for the ancient country of Urartu, where the ark is located at 6,500 feet. The Turkish Government has never issued a dig permit to anyone, even though many applications for an excavation have been submitted. These facts I have taken from https://noahsarkdiscovery.com which shows a number of interesting photos and information confirming this discovery of Noah's Ark, which can also be seen on Google Earth.

I found the website 'Evidence for the Bible' (The Bible | Evidence To Believe) helpful in providing evidence for the accuracy of the Bible. There is confirmation of the Old Testament in hard archaeological evidence. One of the most convincing discoveries was the Dead Sea Scrolls found in Qumran Cave in 1947. There were 223 Qumran manuscripts establishing the reliability of many of the books in the Old Testament: the book of Isaiah found in the Cave, dated 1,000 years earlier than the previously known manuscript (AD 980) and proved to be word for word identical with the standard Hebrew Bible in more than ninety-five per cent of the text. As far as the New Testament is concerned there are 24,970 ancient manuscripts supporting the New Testament. This is far more than any other book of antiquity. The abundance of manuscript copies makes it possible with them to reconstruct the original New Testament with almost complete accuracy.

During the trial of Jesus, Pilate posed an interesting question to Jesus (who did not reply) – "What is truth?" This is a particularly appropriate question for our day and age. Some seem to take the view that getting away with telling a lie is fine. The truth that God the Father expects is personified in Christ Jesus, who stated, *"I am the way and the truth and the life. No-one comes to the Father except through me"* (John 14:6)[1]. As the truth, Christ is the reality of all God's promises. He is the source of truth, setting us free from the consequences of our sins. In speaking about Himself as 'the Son,' He said, *"So if the Son sets you free, you will be free indeed"* (John 8:36). He does not give us freedom so that we can do what we like, but freedom to enable us to follow God.

In some sweet shops there are 'pick and mix' counters to enable customers to select from various containers of different kinds of sweets. Some may adopt this 'pick and mix' approach to the Bible. For instance, many people appreciate God's loving nature but dislike the idea of 'the wrath of God', so satisfy themselves by starting to make up their own 'bespoke God', who is loving but hardly ever angry. Creating a god, by removing what some may regard as negative characteristics, such as God's wrath and judgement, results in a false understanding of the true nature of God. The more we read the Old and New Testaments, the better we will become in knowing God.

The Old Testament prefigures the coming of the Messiah that is documented in the New Testament – 'the Old in the New revealed.' The New Testament often refers back to Old Testament prophecies which have been fulfilled in the Messiah – the Lord Jesus Christ.

The Bible asserts in 2 Timothy 3:16, *'All scripture is God-breathed and is useful for teaching, rebuking,*

---

[1] All scripture quotations in this book (unless otherwise stated) are taken from the 'Life Application Bible (New International Version),' Kingsway Publications, Eastbourne, 1988.

correcting and training in righteousness.' The Holy Spirit revealed God's plan and personality to certain believers, who wrote down these God-breathed messages and events, which were subsequently collected as books in the Bible. These believers were inspired by God and wrote from their own personal, historical and cultural contexts. While using their own minds and talents, they wrote what God wanted them to write. We should read, study and enjoy the Bible, giving thanks and praise to God for revealing Himself to the world through His Son.

2.
Creation

'In the beginning God created the heavens and the earth' (Genesis 1:1). These first words are striking and impressive. A simple statement of fact that should humble us because of the enormity of God's creation. We are part of a vast galaxy and there are over one billion galaxies like ours in the universe.

The rest of Genesis chapter one is an outline of how God created the earth. There is no attempt to explain how God made the universe, no doubt because humanity would be unable to comprehend the complexity of such a task.

What we believe about where we came from effects our views about the meaning of life. Creationists believe that by Jesus Christ, *'all things were created, things in heaven and on earth'* (Colossians 1:16). However, evolutionists believe that life started from a single-celled organism, which over time evolved into complex organisms, even changing into different, distinct animals. Evolution discounts God as Creator, moral Lawgiver and ultimate Judge of all the earth.

Psalm 148:5: *'Let them praise the name of the Lord, for he commanded and they were created.'* When the Bible refers to creation it portrays an instant event, whereas evolutionary theories occur so slowly that their effect is imperceptible to each generation. Consequently, they calculate change over millions of years, to accommodate the concept that living things gradually evolve over time.

Where evolutionists have difficulty is in their suggestion that one species can change to another – such as ape to man – and they are constantly looking for 'the missing link' between animal and man. Genesis 1:21: *'So God created the great creatures of the sea and every living and moving thing with which the water teems, <u>according to their kinds</u>.'* The words that I underlined indicate that living things are made according to their kinds or species, therefore do not evolve from one species to another. The first man, Adam, was no ape or caveman. He was created a mature man, endowed with all the knowledge and skill to perform the tasks that God had assigned him. *'The Lord God took the man* (Adam) *and put him in the Garden of Eden to work it and take care of it.'* (Genesis 2:15). In addition to being a horticulturist, Adam was given the responsibility of naming the different animals. Humanity in Adam was created in the likeness of God in order to be able to respond to God in a mutually loving relationship.

Evolutionists calculate the age of things in many millions of years, when frankly no-one can know what happened that long ago. However, creationists can point to someone who has proved in front of eyewitnesses His authority over creation, especially over 'the elements'.

The Lord Jesus Christ revealed his authority over weather. In Mark 4:35-41, Christ was with his disciples, sleeping in a boat, when a storm nearly capsized the boat. The disciples woke Jesus. *'He got up, rebuked the wind and said to the waves, "Quiet! Be still!" Then the wind died down and it was completely calm.'* The comment by His disciples was, *"Who is this? Even the wind and the waves obey him!"* (Mark 4:41). They were impressed to see the manifested power of the Creator, as He ordered the weather and waves to do His bidding.

In the story of creation (Genesis 1:29) God said to Adam and Eve, *"I give you every seed-bearing plant on the face of the whole earth and every tree that has fruit with seed in it. They will be yours for food."* This would indicate that our early ancestors were vegetarians.

During Christ's ministry, he had a 'run in' with one such fruit bearing tree – a fig tree, which had no fruit. This incident is described in Matthew 21:18-20: *'Early in the morning, as he* (Jesus) *was on his way back to the city, he was hungry. Seeing a fig-tree by the road, he went up to it but found nothing on it except leaves. Then he said to it, "May you never bear fruit again!" Immediately the tree withered. When the disciples saw this, they were amazed. "How did the fig-tree wither so quickly?" they asked.'* The reason the fig-tree withered so quickly was because the One who made it decided that was the moment it should wither. This is another account where there were eyewitnesses to Christ's authority, this time directing the demise of a fruit tree.

In Christ's earthly ministry He also demonstrated that He had power over death by raising three people from the dead, as well as healing many and performing amazing miracles, such as walking on water. Christ had eyewitnesses to all these miracles that revealed His authority over all creation.

The Bible states that Jesus, in co-operation with the Father, created all things. *'He* (Jesus) *is the image of the invisible God, the firstborn over all creation. For by him all things were created: things in heaven and on earth, visible and invisible, whether thrones or powers or rulers or authorities, all things were created by him and for him.'* (Colossians 1:15-16). Being supreme over all creation, Christ can do what He wants, although He willingly submits Himself, and His works, to the Father's will.

3.
Love

Loving God

The Oxford Dictionary describes love as 'an intense feeling of deep affection or fondness'. The Christian definition adds the fact that love comes from God and that Christ reveals the love of God. Love is referred to both in the Old and New Testaments. In the Old Testament, the first four of the Ten Commandments were instructions about loving God, while the remaining six commandments were about how we should love each other.

In the New Testament Christ summarised the commandments as follows: *"Love the Lord your God with all of your heart and with all of your soul and with all of your mind. This is the first and greatest commandment. And the second is like it: Love your neighbour as yourself. All the Law and the Prophets hang on these two commandments."* (Matthew 22:37-40). By fulfilling these two commandments, a person keeps all the others.

I guess the cynic might comment on the commandments, "Easier said than done." Indeed, when first considering Christ's two commandments, one may be struck by the thought, 'It's hard enough trying to love one's neighbour but even harder contemplating loving God, whom we cannot even see.' One aspect of love is getting to know the person, who is the object of our love. Clearly, we need assistance in this and sure enough this is available through the three Persons of the Trinity:

God the Holy Spirit. Christ said, *'But the Counsellor, the Holy Spirit, whom the Father will send in my name, will teach you all things and will remind you of everything I have said to you'* (John 14:26). The Holy Spirit enables us to get to know the Lord Jesus. When in 1978 I was baptised in the Holy Spirit, I experienced a deep sense of love for God, through the ministry of the Holy Spirit, whom at the same time gave me the gift of 'tongues' and prepared me for prison ministry. Encounters like this build up our faith and illuminate our hearts, as we become aware of being in God's presence.

God the Father. Christ said, *'If anyone loves me, he will obey my teaching. My Father will love him, and we will come to him and make our home with him.'* (John 14:23). Love all around! We love Christ. This stimulates the Father to love us and live with us, which in turn becomes a real opportunity for us to get to know God the Father, as well as His Son.

God the Son. Christ came as an exact representation of His Father. Whilst we cannot see God in His full glory, God the Son was seen in human form. Hebrews 1:3: *'The Son is the radiance of God's glory and the exact representation of his being, sustaining all things by his powerful word.'* The more we see God's marvellous attributes in His Son, the more we want to express our love in praise to God the Father.

Taking time to get to know someone requires both commitment and an element of self-discipline. It does not just happen; we need to apply ourselves, especially in our prayer times. On becoming a Christian, we need to be prepared to be disciplined by God to enable us to mature. It is part of sanctification, which involves being made holy through the work of the Holy Spirit. Hebrews 12:6: *'The Lord disciplines those he loves.'*

Christ described our close relationship to Him being like a branch of the Vine (Christ), with the Gardener (the Father) pruning us to ensure stronger growth. Self-discipline and love are both 'fruits' of the Spirit, who provides these to enable Christians to develop perseverance, when subjected to spiritual attack, as well as when disciplined by the Lord.

Loving Others

The apostle who often wrote about love, John, was known as 'the apostle whom Jesus loved' – he was the only apostle who was an eyewitness to the Lord's crucifixion. 2 John 1:5-6 records his words: *'I ask that we love one another. And this is love; that we walk in obedience to his commands. As you have heard from the beginning, his command is that you walk in love.'* We can show love by not judging others: instead accepting, listening, caring and helping people. Our loving actions authenticate our faith in Christ.

Shortly before His crucifixion, Christ prayed to His Father (John 17:22-23). *'I have given them the glory that you gave me, that they may be one as we are one. I in them and you in me. May they be brought to complete unity to let the world know that you sent me and have loved them even as you have loved me.'* The unification of the disciples is a powerful witness to the world.

I am on the mailing list of two Christians organizations who support Christians who are being persecuted – 'Barnabas Fund' and 'Open Doors.' Quite often the prayers for those being persecuted are for courage, faith and unity amongst believers, as this is a perfect witness to their persecutors, sometimes even stimulating them to become Christians. The 'world' is watching the witness of Christians, particularly how they interact with each other.

4.
Why Many Prisoners Show a Positive Response to the Gospel

Incarceration normally produces humility

Whilst 'career offenders' don't particularly mind prison, as it is an 'occupational hazard,' for most imprisonment is a humiliating experience, bringing a recognition of the limitation of personal resources to cope when faced with difficulties. This in turn leads some prisoners to seek a purpose and anchorage in life. This humble attitude towards trials and tribulations produces an openness towards considering new approaches to life.

Christ recognised and acknowledged the rectitude of those who humbly regarded themselves as sinners in need of a Saviour. It is this attitude of openness that pleases Christ, who said, *'It is not the healthy who need a doctor, but the sick. I have not come to call the righteous, but sinners to repentance.'* (Luke 5:31-32). This statement was made in response to a spiteful question put by the Pharisees, who believed they were respectable, when really they had 'hardened hearts' and were very critical of others.

Before being imprisoned, prisoners often feel (like most of us who are at liberty) quite capable of coping through their own strength and abilities. Prison, like any challenging circumstance, often encourages prisoners to develop a more measured and 'healthy' approach to spiritual matters, through acknowledging their personal weaknesses.

Christ had an amazingly humble attitude in that he not only advocated humility, he also modelled this beautiful characteristic in His life. While on earth He laid aside much of His divine power, dying to bring each of us forgiveness of sins. John 12:24 records His words: *'I tell you the truth, unless a grain of wheat falls to the ground and dies, it remains only a single seed. But if it dies, it produces many seeds.'* Unless a kernel of wheat is buried in the ground it will not produce more seeds. Christ died to bring fruitfulness to our lives.

Whilst the Holy Spirit brings an awareness of our weaknesses, it is important to take action on these shortcomings by turning to God for assistance. Sometimes God allows us to come under ever increasing pressure until we suddenly appreciate our need for change. This currently happens to prisoners. It is well described by a psalmist writing about 3000 years ago (Psalm 107:10-16). This passage is appropriate for any who feel 'imprisoned' by their circumstances, as a result of failing to place God first in their lives:

'Some sat in darkness and the deepest gloom, prisoners suffering in iron chains, for they had rebelled against the words of God and despised the counsel of the Most High. So he subjected them to bitter labour; they stumbled, and there was no-one to help. Then they cried to the Lord in their trouble, and he saved them from their distress. He brought them out of darkness and the deepest gloom and broke away their chains. Let them give thanks to the Lord for his unfailing love and his wonderful deeds for men, for

he breaks down gates of bronze and cuts through bars of iron.'

Society labels prisoners as 'offenders', which enables them to acknowledge more easily that they are sinners

Owing to the inherent pride and selfishness in humanity, many find it difficult to accept the concept of 'being sinners'. Many acknowledge that they have done a few misdeeds but believe that generally they live good lives. This is not the case for offenders, who are labelled as such and know that they have done wrong and readily accept their need for forgiveness. Those who fail to acknowledge that they are sinners also fail to grasp the need for a Saviour to bring forgiveness of sins.

I have noticed that sometimes those best at counselling offenders are ex-offenders. In the ex-offender Christian hostels in which I was involved, as offenders grew in their faith, after they left the hostels, several assisted other offenders back to law-abiding lives. One became a minister in the Church of England, while a couple stayed on to become residential staff in our hostels. They were normally readily accepted as counsellors by the residents because they were living examples of how to develop constructive lifestyles. There are a number of fascinating testimonies by former residents of our hostels in my book entitled 'Freedom in Christ', published by Olympia Publishers.

Prisoners have plenty of time to think

About 3500 years ago Moses composed a psalm, which emphasises the need to seriously consider the purpose of life: *'Teach us to number our days aright, that we may gain a heart of wisdom'* (Psalm 90:12). Some years ago, when I visited a prisoner on remand for murder, he told me that while on remand he had become a Christian. About two weeks after his conversion, he was released on bail and murdered. God had given him a 'window of opportunity' to come to faith. We just do not know how long we will live!

In the community people seem content to be 'bombarded' with entertainment on TV and 'captivated' by their mobile phones and computers. This can result in little time for satisfactory relationships with family and friends. People become absorbed with temporal issues, finding it difficult to relax and take the opportunity of meditating on the possibility of eternal existence after this life.

Without mobile phones and limited viewing of the TV, prisoners have more time to think, especially those in 'closed' prisons, where they can be locked up nearly all the time. One of the 'advantages' of being a prisoner is that they become less dependent on gadgets, resulting in more time to think about serious, fundamental questions in life. What should be our purpose in life? Is there an after-life? Is there a God – if there is, what does He want of me? It is when in our more pensive moods that the Holy Spirit has the opportunity to operate in our lives, providing answers to these questions either through the Bible or just in our thoughts.

God encourages us to persist in pursuing Him with these words: *'Seek and you will find'* (Matthew 7:7).

5.
Mens Rea (Guilty Mind)

'Mens rea' is a Latin term about criminal intention. The term refers to the proof required by the prosecution in a criminal court case that the defendant had the intention of committing an offence: in other words, that the defendant had a 'guilty mind.'

I quote a story from the Old Testament in which God appears to hold to this principle of law. Eli was a priest with the task of supervising worship in Israel. His two sons were also priests, who allowed greed, lust and power to get in the way of their communication with God. Eli was aware of his sons' wayward behaviour and made a feeble and unsuccessful attempt to chasten and reform the sons, whose behaviour was undermining the credibility of the priesthood.

God intervened in this serious situation by informing Eli, through the young prophet, Samuel, *'I (God) told him* (Eli) *that I would judge his family for ever because of the* <u>*sin he knew about;*</u> *his sons made themselves contemptible, and he failed to restrain them. Therefore, I swore to the house of Eli, "The guilt of Eli's house will never be atoned for by sacrifice or offering"'* (1 Samuel 3:13-14). Before sentencing Eli's family, God ensured that Eli, and his sons, had a guilty mind (mens rea) – the underlined section in the above scripture passage confirms that Eli did have a guilty mind, knowing his sin of failing to restrain his sons. God's sentence was to refuse to cover (or forgive) by sacrifice the sins of the two sons, who would be punished.

When applying the mens rea to humanity, in terms of having a guilty mind before God for not believing in Him, some might argue that there is an excuse for not believing for those who have never heard about God. However, Paul explains that this is not the case (Romans 1:18-20): *'The wrath of God is being revealed from heaven against all the godlessness and wickedness of men who suppress the truth by their wickedness, since what may be known about God is plain to them, because God has made it plain to them. For since the creation of the world God's invisible qualities – his eternal power and divine nature – have been clearly seen, being understood from what has been made, so that men are without excuse.'* Humanity is without excuse because God has plainly revealed Himself to all people through His creation.

If people suppress the truth by living in wickedness and ignoring the obvious work of the God of creation, they have no excuse for ignoring the truth – even if they live in a tribe without any contact with civilization. Especially in this latter case, missionaries are helpful in pointing out the people's error in not believing the truth about the Creator God and explaining the need for repentance from sin and faith in the Lord Jesus Christ.

In Europe there is only a muted interest in Christianity. People prefer to find contentment in their self-centred lives, so are without excuse for ignoring God. Romans 3:23: *'For all have sinned and fall short of the glory of God.'* Those who fail to repent of sin and turn to Christ as Saviour are disqualified from living with God.

In the UK trivial, temporal things seem to occupy the

attention of many. There is a fascination in the public and private lives of so-called 'celebrities, stars or icons'. Although not a trivial matter, England's great win over Denmark in the 2020 European Soccer Championship semi-finals did not justify the front-page headlines in two national papers, describing the England players as 'demi-gods'. God has placed in the hearts of humanity the desire to worship Him: unfortunately, this desire is often misplaced in adoration of human 'celebrities'.

Covid-19 seems to have been a wake-up call to some, especially those, who in a humble spirit, have acknowledged their need of a Saviour. Perhaps the Holy Spirit is diverting people away from depression and self-doubt into 'true hero worship' of the Lord Jesus Christ, who is in the image of God, as well as 'the Way' back to God. In discussion with His disciples, the Lord Jesus Christ said, *'I am the way and the truth and the life. No-one comes to the Father except through me. If you really knew me, you would know my Father as well. From now on, you do know him and have seen him'* (John 14:6-7). Jesus is the way to the Father, the truth, as He reveals what the Father is like, and the life, in that He joins His divine life to ours, now and throughout eternity.

This closeness of the Son to the Father is particularly apparent in Jesus' prayer to the Father, shortly before His death: *'Now this is eternal life: that they may know you, the only true God, and Jesus Christ, whom you have sent'* (John 17:3). Knowing God, through Christ, is central to the Christian faith.

6.
Challenging the Strange Fascination in Horoscopes

Most of the points made in the first four paragraphs of this article are taken from Wikipedia. Western astrology is a form of divination based on horoscopes for an exact moment, such as a person's birthday. Most current horoscopes are based on sun sign astrology, which is a pseudoscience that claims to divine information about human events and terrestrial events by studying the position of celestial objects. It is purported that horoscopes explain aspects of someone's personality.

Researchers have successfully challenged astrology and shown it to have no scientific validity or explanatory power. Horoscopes often refer to an astrologer's interpretation based on the position of the sun at time of birth, or on the calendar significance of an event. Many newspapers and magazines carry predictive columns, written more for increasing readership than tied to the sun or other aspects of the solar system. Birth charts, or zodiac signs, are often used to predict a person's personality traits.

In research studies one astrologer's prediction for a horoscope is typically unrelated to the prediction of another astrologer. Horoscopes often have general and vague wording, based on typical everyday events, and this may account for the many who believe their horoscopes align to the events in their lives. Gallup Polls taken in Britain, Canada and the USA between 1975 and 1996 asked the question, 'Do you believe in horoscopes?', to which twenty-five per cent of adults polled 'yes'.

The Christian view is that horoscopes or the practice of astrology should not be used. The late evangelist and minister, Billy Graham, said, 'God did make the stars (as well as everything in the universe), but He intended them to be a witness to His power and glory, not as a means to guide us or foretell the future.'

Today people are fascinated by horoscopes, fortune-telling, witchcraft, astronomy and the occult. This interest can be due to curiosity or a desire to know and control the future. We need to accept that God will tell us all that we need to know about our future, so we don't need the occult, which utilises supernatural beliefs and practices that fall outside the scope of religion and science. There are several references in the Bible forbidding any involvement in the occult. For example, Isaiah, an Old Testament prophet, made the following prophecy, in which he was speaking on behalf of God: *'All the counsel you have received has only worn you out! Let your astrologers come forward, those stargazers who make predictions month by month, let them save you from what is coming upon you'* (Isaiah 47:13).

The acid test of any prophecy or prediction is whether or not it comes to pass. I imagine that because many of the horoscope predictions are so vague and nebulous, some might claim that the horoscopes are true for them but, as explained in the second paragraph above, these predictions cannot be validated by researchers. Therefore, it is hard to understand why one in four of us believe in horoscopes.

Using the acid test of accuracy, it would make more sense if people believed the Bible, which is full of prophecies that have come true, some in minute detail, thousands of years after the prophecies.

A good example of accurate prophecy is Psalm 22, written over 1,000 years before the event, by King David, described as 'a man after God's own heart'. This description of David's character is illustrated in Psalm 22 through some of the events he predicted about Christ's crucifixion. The graphic details give a sense of David actually feeling Christ's agony and loneliness during His dying hours.

There are several accurate prophecies in this psalm but I will specifically just consider three:

Prophecy. Psalm 22:1: *'My God, my God, why have you forsaken me?'*

Fulfilment in Christ's words. Matthew 27:46 and Mark, 15:34: *'My God, my God, why have you forsaken me?'*

Prophecy. Psalm 22:8: *'He trusts in the Lord; let the Lord rescue him. Let him deliver him, since he delights in him.'*

Fulfilment in words of those mocking Christ. Matthew 27:43: *'He trusts in God. Let God rescue him now, if he wants him, for he said, "I am the Son of God".'*

Prophecy. Psalm 22:18: *'They divide my garments among them and cast lots for my clothing.'*

Fulfilment in the actions and words of the soldiers, who crucified Christ. John 19:23-24: *'When the soldiers crucified Jesus, they took his clothes, dividing them into four shares, one for each of them, with the undergarment remaining. This garment was seamless, woven in one piece from top to bottom. "Let's not tear it," they said to one another. "Let's decide by lot who will get it."'*

The last prophecy fulfilment about dividing Christ's clothes by lot is recorded in all four gospels. However, John's recollection (above) of this event is more detailed, as he was the only one of the apostles who was an eye-witness to the crucifixion.

Another amazing prophecy from the Old Testament was made by the prophet Isaiah about 150 years before its fulfilment. Isaiah, speaking on behalf of God, even mentioned the name ('Cyrus') of the person who would fulfil the prophecy. (Isaiah 44:28): *"Cyrus, 'He is my shepherd and will accomplish all that I* (God) *please; he will say of Jerusalem, "Let it be rebuilt", and of the temple, "Let its foundation be laid".'"* Cyrus was the powerful, secular king of Persia in BC 559, who had conquered much of the world, including Israel, most of whose inhabitants had been deported from Israel. However, it is thought that Cyrus was so moved when he read the prophecy that he carried it out by allowing those captive Jews who wanted to rebuild the temple to leave Persia to return to Jerusalem for this purpose.

The following proclamation (Ezra 1:2-3) constitutes the fulfilment of Isaiah's prophecy: *'This is what Cyrus king of Persia says, "The Lord, the God of heaven, has given me all the kingdoms of the earth and he has appointed me to build a temple for him at Jerusalem in Judah. Anyone of his people among you – may his God be with him, and let him go up to Jerusalem in Judah to build the temple of the Lord, the God of Israel, the God who is in Jerusalem."'*

I leave the last word on this subject to the Lord Jesus, who told the Jews, *"If you hold to my teaching, you are really my disciples. Then you will know the truth, and the truth will set you free"* (John 8:31-32). Rather than becoming reliant on horoscopes, believe on Christ's proven words of truth and freedom, *"So if the Son sets you free, you will be free indeed"* (John 8:36).

7.
Tackling Addictions

Paul wrote (1 Corinthians 6:12), *'"Everything is permissible for me" – but not everything is beneficial. "Everything is permissible to me" – but I will not be mastered by anything.'* The problem with nearly all addictions is that they master the addict, although the addict will seldom admit this. Some actions, like drinking alcohol, are not sinful in themselves, when taken in moderation. However, regular excessive consumption becomes an addiction, which in extreme cases can control a person's life with devastating consequences. It is worth considering some of the facts about the more common addictions in the UK.

Alcoholism. In 2020 in the UK, 8.4 million people showed signs of alcohol dependence. The effects of alcohol are detrimental to physical and mental health. The Office for National Statistics said that in 2008 there were 9,031 alcohol-related deaths in England and Wales. Alcohol-related admissions to hospital have risen by more than two-thirds in a decade; in 2017 admissions were 1.1 million, according to data released by Public Health England.

I was involved with a charity called Stepping Stones Trust, whose services have since been taken over by a large Christian charity. Our first hostel in London provided Christian care mainly for ex-prisoners with alcohol addictions. One of the residents had committed a number of alcohol-related convictions. He settled in well to the hostel and became a Christian. The local link church with the hostel provided sensitive and helpful support. He spiritually matured and was appointed a curate in the church. Subsequently, he became a Church of England minister. Sadly, when in his first parish, he returned to alcoholism and while in custody in Brixton Prison hung himself.

It is important to recognise that while addictive behaviour may be on the wane for several years, there is always a chance of it returning when least expected. While in 'recovery mode', there can be a feeling of elation at successfully tackling the addiction; however, care needs to be taken because of the propensity for demonic powers to be 'prowling' around waiting to attack. This is similar to a lion chasing a pack of deer, waiting to assault the weakest animal at the back of the pack. 1 Peter 5:8-9: *'Be self-controlled and alert. Your enemy the devil prowls around like a roaring lion looking for someone to devour. Resist him, standing firm in the faith, because you know that your brothers throughout the world are undergoing the same kind of sufferings.'*

Drug Misuse. The UK has the highest prevalence of drug misuse in Europe, with about one third of adults in England and Wales reported to have used drugs at least once in their lifetime. The Office for National Statistics reported that in England and Wales in 2020 there were 4,561 drug related deaths. This was the eighth successive year that deaths increased. In 2020 in Scotland there were 1,339 drug related deaths, which was the seventh year that deaths increased.

I supervised many drug addicts, and sadly some died very lonely people. Near the end of their lives the only thing that mattered was the next 'fix'. It can be really hard to wean a drug user from his preferred illegal drugs and also from his dependence on his drug-taking friends. The three illegal drugs, which I found were particularly destructive, were LSD, crack cocaine and heroin.

1) LSD is a hallucinogenic drug which has the effect of altering thoughts, feelings, and awareness of one's surroundings. Many users have visual or auditory hallucinations. One such example was a client on LSD wanting to throw himself out of a window, as he believed he could fly.

2) Crack cocaine is a very dangerous drug, as it puts a great strain on the heart and central nervous system, sometimes leading to depression and suicide. One of the main side effects of this drug is violence.

3) Heroin addiction was quite common when I worked in Richmond, as the town was close to a drug treatment centre in Kingston, Surrey. The centre concentrated on providing methadone, which is an opioid medication that reduces withdrawal symptoms in people addicted to heroin. Heroin addicts would congregate near the treatment centre and after having collected their methadone, some would commit further offences to 'fuel' their addiction. Quite often heroin addicts successfully stopped using heroin by using methadone but subsequently became addicted to methadone, very occasionally for as long as thirty years.

After several of my clients informed me that they had first taken drugs while in custody, I wanted to find out why drugs were easily obtained in some prisons, so I asked this question to a long-time drug supplier client of mine. He told me that drugs were usually smuggled into prison by putting them in a cellophane package and then up the rectum. Apparently, because EU laws forbade personally intrusive searches, this meant that the rectum could not be searched. I was concerned that a couple of my clients were coming under the temptation to start drug-taking due to this systemic prison failure. I informed the Health Secretary, who informed the Home Office, who said they could do nothing to stop this 'racket'. Now that the UK has left the EU, maybe the potential for this unhealthy and illegal drug smuggling could be re-examined.

Gambling. There are estimated to be 430,000 problem gamblers in the UK, the number of eleven to sixteen-year-old children who were classified as problem gamblers being 55,000. It is estimated that gambling addiction costs the UK around £600 million per annum. The gambling industry in total in 2020 was worth £14.3 billion and employed over 98,000 people. It is estimated that only about five per cent of compulsive gamblers seek help from a gambling programme or gambling rehabilitation centres, leaving ninety-five per cent of problem gamblers with lives ruined by debt and depression.

I believe it is important to acknowledge having an addiction of any sort because until the addiction is acknowledged, support and guidance cannot be effectively offered. 'Alcoholics Anonymous' have the right idea in expecting those who use their organization to admit they have a compulsive addiction to alcohol.

For a short while in the early 1970s I was virtually a gambling addict. I had inherited money, which I unwisely 'moved around' the Stock Market. When the stocks were 'flying high' I was happy, but when the FTSE dropped, so did my feeling of elation. Christ accurately summed up my position when he said, *'For where your treasurer is, there your heart will be also'* (Matthew 6:21). I had become a slave to the Stock Market. With the help of my wife and my faith, I was able 'to walk away' from this addiction but am aware that I need to be careful to avoid any potential temptations to gamble.

The greedy longings of the mind (addictions) are powerful but as we become aware of our inability to control these, we need to humbly seek God's consolation and guidance in tackling our weaknesses. It is pointless trying to hide our inner selves from the all-seeing and all-knowing God. I will end with an extract from the apostle John's letter (1 John 2:15-17): *'Do not love the world or anything in the world. If anyone loves the world, the love of the Father is not in him. For everything in the world – the cravings of sinful man, the lust of his eyes and the boasting of what he has and does – comes not from the Father but from the world. The world and its desires pass away, but the man who does the will of God lives for ever.'*

8.
Abominable Abortion

Abortion is the termination of a pregnancy by the removal or expulsion of an embryo or foetus. When deliberate steps are taken to end a pregnancy, this is usually called an induced abortion. The 1967 Abortion Act has been in operation for fifty-three years and the latest approximate figure of lives lost through abortion is 9.7 million (January 2022). Following are some concerning statistics from 'Right to Life' News:

In England and Wales, an unborn baby is aborted every three minutes.

Over sixty per cent of England's abortion clinics are rated inadequate or require improvement when it comes to safety.

25.2% of pregnancies in 2019 in England and Wales now ends in abortion, according to the Office of National Statistics.

One of the main arguments for the initial introduction of the Abortion Act was concern about the risk to the mother due to the unsafe clinics undertaking abortions. It is a serious flaw in the oversight and management of abortions that after fifty-three years in operation, sixty per cent of the abortion clinics are inadequate or require improvement when it comes to safety. With 9.7 million abortions since the enactment of the 1967 Abortion Act, it is a shame on our country that we have slaughtered more unborn babies than the combined populations of the whole of London and Bristol (using the 2017 population estimates).

This dreadful practice of sacrificing our children is forbidden in the Bible. 2 Chronicles 28:1-3 recounts how Ahaz, King of Judah, sacrificed his sons in the fire and this was regarded as detestable. About 3,500 years ago the Lord gave Moses these instructions to pass on to the Israelites: *'Any Israelite or any alien living in Israel who gives any of his children to Molech must be put to death'* (Leviticus 20:2). This is a reference to child sacrifice, which was common practice in ancient religions. God was warning His people not to follow the practice of the Ammonite tribe, who sacrificed their children to their national god, Molech, to ward off evil or appease angry gods.

Although we currently live in a civilised society, our practice of slaughtering innocent, vulnerable, little babies through abortion is far from civilised, revealing that in this matter we are little more advanced than our ancestors, who lived 3,500 years ago. The right of life for the unborn baby should outweigh the right of a mother over the control of her own body. A significant danger in having an abortion is that it can damage the long-term emotional health of women.

When examining the statistics in paragraph one and two (above) we need to be realists. This Abortion Act has now gone way beyond the legislators' original intentions, with over one in four pregnancies ending in abortion in England and Wales.

While I don't know how far the pro-abortion lobby are engaged in what would be a useful exercise in seeking to improve the current inadequate abortion clinics, their 'direction of travel' has recently been exposed by their actions. On 5 July 2021, they tabled for debate in the House of Commons an extreme abortion amendment to the Police, Crime, Sentencing and Courts Bill, decriminalising abortion up to birth.

The Christian charity 'Care' mobilised support against this amendment, which 'Care' explained if passed, 'would be the last remaining legal protection for preborn babies, raise the upper limit on abortion from twenty-four weeks to birth, and open the door to sex-selective abortion.' 'Care' advised its members to contact their local MPs, which I did. Apparently, many others also approached their MPs, some of whom spoke powerfully against this amendment, which fortunately was withdrawn. However, within a few years, no doubt another attempt at passing this amendment will be made.

Abortion affected a couple of my clients. Shortly after the Abortion Act became operational, an abortion clinic was opened near where I worked. In the early 1970s two of the medical staff in the clinic became clients of mine. Both told me of their depression brought about by the expectation by management that they dispose of the bodies of unborn babies. They were upset because they realised that the aborted babies were not just a bundle of flesh but moving, active little beings. The two medical staff had become very depressed due to their working environment, which I regarded was one of the crime causations factors behind their offending. If these two medical staff found it difficult working in an abortion clinic fifty years ago, imagine the additional emotional pressure on abortion clinic staff if the pro-abortion lobby successfully push through legislation to decriminalise abortion up to birth.

I had to prepare a social enquiry report for court on a female client, who at the time was on remand in Holloway Prison. Her offences included burglary and other drug related offences. She had had an unhappy childhood; by the time she was aged seventeen years she had had three abortions, which created further depression. Whilst on remand in custody she became a Christian. On release I supervised her and she settled down well. After her supervision finished, I kept in contact with her on a voluntary basis for about twenty-five years, mainly through the exchange of Christmas cards, so I was aware of her progress. She successfully brought up three of her own children, acknowledging the importance of providing them with happy, fulfilling lives rather than destroying them through abortion.

'He (Christ) *is the image of the invisible God, the firstborn over all creation. For by him all things were created: things in heaven and on earth, visible and invisible, whether thrones or powers or rulers or authorities; all things were created by him and for him'* (Colossians 1:15-16). The centrality of the Christian faith is the deity of Christ, who is supreme over His creation. He gives us many good gifts in life, one of the best being our children. We should respect and not destroy His good gifts.

9.
Humility Trumps Pride

Pride

Humility is the opposite to pride, which is revealed in an arrogant feeling of importance due to a person's achievements, status or profession. Pride is a pretence of having a greatness and glory that actually belong to God. Scripture often speaks of how God humbles the proud, who had become self-centred, demonstrating a greedy, grasping attitude towards what can be seen, touched, or imagined.

Pride is personified in Satan. The Biblical teaching of his early history is that God created the hosts of heaven, mainly composed of angels, one of whom was Lucifer (known as Satan). The latter became 'big headed', and had grandiose ideas about becoming like God. His pride could not be tolerated by God, so war broke out in heaven (Revelations chapter 12). Satan and his compatriots, one third of the heavenly hosts, were 'hurled down to the earth' (Revelations 12:9). Pride literally resulted in a major fall for Satan. *'Pride goes before destruction, a haughty spirit before a fall'* (Proverbs 16:18). Proud people think that they are above the frailties of others; in this state of mind, they are easily tripped up. *'The Lord detests all the proud of heart. Be sure of this. They will not go unpunished'* (Proverbs 16:5).

While pride is generally easy to detect, there are some

less obvious manifestations of it in our society, in which people want to be seen, noticed and applauded. So-called 'celebrities' desire 'visibility', especially through TV and social media. This satisfies their desire for self-aggrandisement; good deeds and achievements are advertised in order to receive recognition, fame and fortune. This proud attitude is quite the reverse to that which Jesus advocated, *'Be careful not to do your "acts of righteousness" before men, to be seen by them. If you do, you will have no reward from your Father in heaven'* (Matthew 6:1). He wanted to divert attention away from people seeking praise from each other, by advocating the value in seeking to obtain God's praise. *'How can you believe if you accept praise from one another, yet make no effort to obtain the praise that comes from the only God'* (John 5:44).

What really angers God is when a man claims to be a god. When this occurs God swiftly judges the person concerned. In the Old Testament it was recorded that this happened to the ruler of Tyre, the capital of Phoenicia, just north of Israel. Tyre and Judah both competed for the lucrative trade that came through their lands from Egypt in the South. Consequently, Tyre rejoiced when Judah was defeated.

Ezekiel, a prophet in the Old Testament, spoke the following prophecy (Ezekiel 28:1-2): *'The word of the Lord came to me: "Son of man, say to the ruler of Tyre, 'This is what the Sovereign Lord says: In the pride of your heart you say, "I am a god; I sit on the throne of a god in the heart of the seas." But you are a man and not a god, though you think you are as wise as a god'."'* 'Sitting on the throne of a god in the heart of the seas' refers to Tyre's good location as a trading sea port. Some years later Ezekiel's prophecy was fulfilled when the city was captured by an invading army.

Humility

Jesus told His disciples, *'Blessed are the poor in spirit, for theirs is the kingdom of heaven'* (Matthew 5:3). The Amplified Bible explains that the 'poor in spirit' are those who are 'humble, rating themselves as insignificant.' Humility is an attitude of lowliness and obedience, based on the recognition of our true status before God as His children.

There was an incident related in the Bible (Luke chapter 9:43-48) when Christ warned his disciples that He would be betrayed. At the time they did not seem to understand what He was talking about. It is recorded that immediately after Christ's sombre statement, instead of showing any concern towards their master's future, the disciples started an argument amongst themselves about whom would be the greatest.

With Christ's flair for practical illustrations, He responded to His disciple's insensitivity by beautifully illustrating His teaching on humility. Matthew 18:1-4: *'At that time the disciples came to Jesus and asked, "Who is the greatest in the kingdom of heaven?" He called a little child and had him stand among them. And he said: "I tell you the truth, unless you change and become like little children, you will never enter the kingdom of heaven. Therefore, whoever humbles himself like this child is the greatest in the kingdom of heaven."'* Jesus used the child to illustrate that His disciples should not be childish in seeking advantageous positions but instead become childlike, with humble and sincere hearts.

In the Bible the clashing worldly value to pride is humility. The latter has the big advantage that God provides grace to the humble, whereas He opposes the proud. *"God opposes the proud but gives grace to the humble"* (James 4:6).

10.
The Lost

In Luke chapter 15 Jesus relates three parables about a lost sheep, coin and son. When we lose something, our first reaction may be to panic. This was not the case in the two parables involving a lost sheep and coin. Instead of panic, Jesus explained how there was an orderly search for what was lost. The shepherd carefully put his other sheep aside while he searched, until he found his single, lost sheep. While the woman who lost one of her ten silver coins organised a spring-clean of her house. Palestinian women used to receive ten silver coins as a wedding gift, so retaining the complete set of ten rings would have held sentimental importance for her.

In the third parable no search was involved. The father acceded to his younger son's arrogant request for his share (probably one-third) of the estate. The father showed wisdom and restraint in not chasing after his son to try to dissuade him from leaving. The son subsequently spent his inheritance on 'wild living'.

Jesus always seemed to tailor his talks to reach specific people. The listeners to these parables were from two very different groups. One group were Pharisees and teachers of the law, who would not normally associate with the other group of listeners, who were tax collectors and 'sinners'. As Jesus' discourse progressed the former group grew uncomfortable due to Jesus' apparent preference and tenderness towards the 'sinners group'.

The woman's response to finding her lost coin was touching in that she encouraged her friends and neighbours to rejoice over her discovery. On finding the lone sheep, the shepherd responded in the same way, telling his friends and neighbours to, *'Rejoice with me* (Jesus)*; I have found my lost sheep. I tell you that in the same way there will be more rejoicing in heaven over one sinner who repents than over ninety-nine righteous persons who do not need to repent'* (Luke 15:6-7). In the case of the return of his lost son, the father showed ecstatic joy by gathering his household for a welcome home party for the prodigal son. The purpose in these parables was to show that there was great rejoicing in heaven over a sinner who repents.

Jesus subtly challenged the disparate spirit of his audience. The 'sinner group' must have rejoiced at the father's treatment of the prodigal son, as it gave them hope of being accepted by Jesus. Whereas the Pharisee group were mainly looking to find fault in Jesus to justify their murderous opposition against Him. Jesus was aware that the Pharisees wrapped their sin in respectability by pretending to be good and pointing out the sins of others. Jesus said in an earlier encounter with them, *'It is not the healthy who need a doctor, but the sick, I have not come to call the righteous, but sinners to repentance'* (Luke 5:31-32). Jesus chose to give time to those who were aware of their own sin and knew they were not good enough for God – those Jesus described as the sick. He had little time for the self-righteous religious leaders, whom he described as 'the righteous'.

The parable of the lost sheep is about God's search for repentant sinners. It is comforting to know that God's love for each of us is so great that He seeks out each one, rejoicing when the person is "found". The Good Shepherd is happy to associate with sinners – people regarded by others as beyond help.

Some in the churches are not too keen to associate with those they regard as unworthy to come into church. An ex-prisoner told me that soon after his release he wanted to grow in his Christian faith, so went into the first church he could find. After sitting down in a pew, a sidesman told him to leave the church as he was wearing jeans – unacceptable in church! This little incident mirrors the issue that Jesus was up against with the self-satisfied attitude of the Pharisees.

In the parable of the lost son, a Jew, would have felt very humiliated feeding pigs, as Jews did not even touch pigs. He had resorted to undertaking this work after spending his entire inheritance. Having presumably sunk to the depth of depression, this enabled him to come to his senses. Up until this time he was just able to cope, but feeding pigs – no!

The older son in the third parable was jealous of the attention given to his younger, wayward brother, so complained to his father, who showed the same sensitivity and compassion to both sons. The father must have been constantly waiting for his younger son because as soon as the son appeared on the horizon, the father, who had been waiting and looking out for him, rushed out and hugged him. How he must have loved his son in showing such self-control and wisdom in not trying to dissuade the younger son from leaving home. Whilst he assured the older son 'everything I have is yours', it must have been distressing for the father to see the critical, jealous spirit in his older son and heir, who should have been rejoicing with the rest of the household over the return of his younger brother.

In 1975, I supervised my first Christian client and tried hard to enable him to become independent, find employment and suitable lodgings. After the expiry of his probation order, I kept in contact with him on a voluntary basis, even occasionally taking him to church. I began to realise that when he was in difficulty, I was unhelpfully 'cushioning' him from reality. I tended to take the strain, when it should have been taken by him. I told him that I was stopping his voluntary supervision, so he could no longer turn to me for assistance and advice. For a while he lived as a homeless alcoholic, until, like the prodigal son, he was enlightened by the Holy Spirit and through his own initiative broke out of his cycle of prison and homelessness.

God, the compassionate Father, is still eagerly waiting for the return of prodigal sons.

Part 2
Christians

This section is mainly written for Christians. For additional information on Christian counselling on 'How to become a Christian' and 'Counselling a Believer in the Baptism of the Holy Spirit', see my book 'Freedom for Prisoners' published by Olympia Publishers.

11.
The Theocratic Disciplined Exodus

The Israelites were slaves for 400 years in Egypt, where they were cruelly oppressed. They prayed for deliverance to God, who answered by appointing Moses as their leader and through him rescued the nation in about 1280 BC: the exodus from Egypt involved around two million people.

At the time the form of government God instituted among the Israelites was a theocracy, in which God was the supreme ruler and gave them laws based on the Ten Commandments. These days it is hard to imagine how God took personal control of a nation and physically led them. *'By day the Lord went ahead of them* (the Israelites) *in a pillar of cloud to guide them on their way and by night in a pillar of fire to give them light, so that they could travel by day or night'* (Exodus 13:21).

It must have been a massive logistical headache to take such a huge group around a desert for forty years. God arranged for them to have daily manna for bread: when they wanted meat, he arranged for them to eat quail (a small migratory bird). *'During the forty years that I* (God) *led you through the desert, your clothes did not wear out, nor did the sandals on your feet. You ate no bread and drank no wine or other fermented drink. I did this so that you might know that I am the Lord your God.'* (Deuteronomy 29:5-6). God personally looked after the Israelites on a daily basis in the hope that they might recognise, love and obey Him as God.

It must have been frustrating for God that despite His kindness in releasing His people from slavery and nurturing them as they wandered through the desert, they generally failed to respond in obedience and gratitude to his miraculous power and love. At the start of this long journey, He had marched the nation through the Red Sea and destroyed the pursuing Egyptian Army. The response of the Israelites to these amazing miracles was to disobey God and grumble against Moses. The people even made a golden calf as an idol to worship, while Moses was receiving God's Law on Mount Sinai. This indifference to God's goodness seems to have continued in humanity's DNA until the present time.

To keep order amongst this unruly crowd required discipline, otherwise anarchy would have erupted: at one point it almost did break out when the people rebelled, saying to each other, *'We should choose a leader and go back to Egypt'* (Numbers 14:4). God threatened to destroy the Israelites, but was dissuaded from this course of action by Moses, with his compelling argument that as the Egyptians knew that God was with the Israelites, if God destroyed them in the desert, the Egyptians and surrounding nations around would say, *'The Lord was not able to bring these people into the land he promised them on oath; so he slaughtered them in the desert.'* (Numbers 14:16). In relenting of this action, God revealed patience and mercy in forgiving His people and even being prepared to change His plan as a result of Moses' skilled advocacy.

Despite a close relationship with Moses, when the latter

did not fully comply with one of God's instructions, He directed that Moses would not enter the 'Promised Land'. As Moses represented God, it was unacceptable for him to deviate from God's directions. In this theocratic government, discipline was vital for the good of God's people.

God is the same yesterday, today and forever – He does not change. However, what does sometimes need to change is our attitude, so that we can become sufficiently humble to accept being disciplined. *'My son, do not make light of the Lord's discipline, and do not lose heart when he rebukes you, because the Lord disciplines those he loves, and he punishes everyone he accepts as a son.'* (Hebrews 12:5-6). As a Father to His people, God did not want them harmed so taught them what was right, even though His discipline was sometimes hard to accept.

Although Moses was refused permission to enter the Promised Land with the Israelites, in God's rich mercy He allowed Moses to enter the land about 1,500 years later, when he and Elijah were seen by three disciples talking to Jesus on the 'Mount of Transfiguration' (Matthew 17:1-13).

Returning to the story of the Exodus, it did not take long for the Israelites to reach Kadesh, from where Moses sent out spies into the 'Promised Land' (the territory of the Canaanite nations). Two of the spies, Joshua and Caleb, provided a favourable minority report, encouraging the Israelites to capture the land, whilst the majority of spies advised against entering the land.

God was very angry with the people for their lack of faith to trust Him to ensure they captured the Promised Land, which He had previously promised to Abraham and his descendants. God had disciplined Moses for his failure to fully obey God on one occasion, now God had to harshly discipline His wayward nation, for their lack of faith in this matter, as well as their persistent grumbling against Him and Moses during the journey. His punishment is recorded in Numbers 14:29-30: *'In this desert your bodies will fall – every one of you twenty years old or more who was counted in the census and who has grumbled against me. Not one of you will enter the land I swore with uplifted hand to make your home, except Caleb son of Jephunneh and Joshua son of Nun.'* God added forty years onto their wanderings to give sufficient time for the fulfilment of His sentence on the rebellious Israelites.

Under the courageous leadership of Joshua, the Israelites did eventually capture most of the Promised Land. In failing to capture the whole land as directed by God, this resulted in some of the Israelites turning to worship the gods of the surviving Canaanite tribes. Many years later Israel split in two and both halves were captured at different times: the Northern half by the Assyrians and later, the Southern half by the Babylonians. This is yet another illustration of a disciplined God requiring love and obedience from His people. When this is not forth coming, 'the cause and effect' principle becomes operative – rebellion against God ultimately leads to God's inevitable discipline and punishment.

12.
The Battle for the Mind

When troops capture a piece of ground, like a hill, they occupy it quickly using the defensive positions, which they had just captured. They need to act fast because normally the enemy will mount a swift counter-attack to try to retrieve their former positions. The counter-attacking forces have one advantage in that they are aware of the weak spots in the defences, as they formerly occupied those defences.

We are involved in a spiritual conflict (Ephesians 6:12), *'For our struggle is not against flesh and blood, but against the rulers, against the authorities, against the powers of this dark world and against the spiritual forces of evil in the heavenly realms.'* Those who are described as 'not flesh and blood' are demons, whose aim is to defeat Christ's Church. The battle is largely fought in the mind against the demonic forces, who, before we were Christians, had easy access to our minds. Hence, after a person becomes a Christian, with a new occupying force in the mind (the Holy Spirit), demonic forces are likely to counter attack through our weaknesses, of which they are aware.

When unsure about how to proceed in any new venture, it is best to ask, 'How would Christ have dealt with this new challenge?' This can only be effective with careful study of Christ's life, especially His encounters with people. At Christ's baptism God the Father 'commissioned' His Son for ministry with these words: *'You are my Son, whom I love; with you I am well pleased'* (Luke 3:22). The Holy Spirit then led the Lord into the desert, where He fasted for forty days before being tempted.

We can learn to resist temptation by following Christ's example. Each of the three times Christ was tempted He responded to Satan by using scripture, which is called the 'Sword of the Spirit'. One might think that Satan would not be particularly interested in scripture: however, he knows scripture well as he previously resided in heaven. Originally, he was an angel but after he and a third of the angels rebelled against God, they were all thrown out of heaven onto Earth. As an angel, Satan, as well as other demonic spirits, would have known Christ. This is apparent from several of Christ's encounters with demons, whose first remarks to Christ were that they knew He was the Son of God.

Christ's answer to the third and last temptation was, *'Away from me, Satan! For it is written: "Worship the Lord your God, and serve him only"'* (Matthew 4:10). In following Christ's example, strengthened by the Holy Spirit's power, we can resist temptations from demonic spirits in the same way as Jesus did and follow the advice in James 4:7: *'Submit yourselves, then, to God. Resist the devil, and he will flee from you.'*

As we are involved in a spiritual battle, like a soldier who 'wants to please his commanding officer' (2 Timothy 2:4), we need to be trained for battle. When I was serving as a Captain in a mechanised infantry regiment in the 'British Army on the Rhine', my commanding officer recognised the value of physical fitness so told me to arrange orientation competitions for the 600 men of the regiment. I arranged for the soldiers to run in orientation competitions almost every day of the week for several months so eventually they became quite fit – particularly the cooks!

I followed my commanding officer's orders, as I wanted to please him. However, the Bible says, *'For physical training is of some value, but godliness has value for all things, holding promise for both the present life and the life to come'* (1 Timothy 4:8). We spend much time on physical fitness but spiritual exercise (godliness) is more important.

As Christians, because our commanding officer is Christ, we should seek to please Him by keeping spiritually fit. Here are some relevant scriptures for our spiritual training. Before starting it is important to take our 'spiritual temperature'. Paul explains how this is done (Romans 8:5): *'Those who live according to the sinful nature have their minds set on what that nature desires; but those who live in accordance with the Spirit have their minds set on what the Spirit desires.'* Without becoming too introspective, assess what you have been thinking about in the last few hours. If you have been concentrating on an important task at work or at home, that's fine, but when you have time to think at leisure, is your mind set on what the Spirit desires? Sadly, we tend to depend too much on being entertained, watching TV, social media or other internet sites, which is not always wholesome for the mind.

Christ said, *'For out of the heart come evil thoughts, murder, adultery, sexual immorality, theft, false testimony, slander'* (Matthew 15:19). This is the most profound and accurate crime causation statement ever made. The 'heart' is the essence of what we are deep down in the core of our being. We need to train our minds to avoid evil thoughts, which are often implanted in us by demonic opposition. We only sin if we cherish or continue to entertain these thoughts. At 'new birth' we receive a 'spiritual heart transplant'. This does not mean that we never sin again – of course we will, but the difference is that we begin to sense that we are no longer in 'slavery to sin' and evil thoughts, which in extreme cases can lead to the commission of serious offences as recorded in Matthew 15:19.

Much spiritual training is progressive, requiring perseverance, as explained in Romans 12:2: *'Do not conform any longer to the pattern of this world, but be transformed by the renewing of your mind. Then you will be able to test and approve what God's will is – his good, pleasing and perfect will.'* We need to refuse to conform to some of this world's values and ensure that our minds are transformed and renewed to enable us to live to honour and obey God, being able to discern His good and perfect will.

13.
Dealing With Depression

The 'Office for National Statistics' indicates that depression has dramatically increased during the Covid-19 pandemic. Prior to Covid-19, ten per cent of adults experienced some form of depression, whilst in early 2021 this figure had more than doubled to twenty-one per cent.

In the Old Testament, it is recorded how God counselled one of His prophets, who suddenly became very depressed after he was threatened with death. 1 Kings 18 describes how God worked an overwhelming miracle through Elijah in defeating (by slaughtering) 450 pagan prophets of Baal. Queen Jezebel retaliated by threatening to kill Elijah. In 1 Kings chapter 19 it is recorded that Elijah felt afraid, depressed, suicidal and abandoned, so ran off.

There followed an interesting counselling process that God undertook with Elijah:

Through the ministry of an angel, God dealt with Elijah's symptoms of depression – lack of sleep and appetite. Elijah had told God, 'I have had enough, Lord,' he (Elijah) said. 'Take my life; I am no better than my ancestors.' Then he lay down under the tree and fell asleep. All at once an angel touched him and said, 'Get up and eat.' (1 Kings 19:4-5). The angel then provided the necessary food.

1 Kings 19:9-10: *'And the word of the Lord came to him: "What are you doing here, Elijah?" He replied, "I have been very zealous for the Lord God Almighty. The Israelites have rejected your covenant, broken down your altars, and put your prophets to death with the sword. I am the only one left, and now they are trying to kill me too."'*

At that stage God did not comment on Elijah's answer. God's next move was probably designed to shake Elijah out of his negative, depressive state. God revealed His glory and power in an audio-visual display with a hurricane, earthquake, fire and finally through 'a gentle whisper'. To test out the effect of this manifestation of God's glory to Elijah, after the display, a voice asked him the same question a second time: *'What are you doing here, Elijah?'* (1 Kings 19:13). Rather than expressing the thrill of seeing God's glory, Elijah seemed unmoved, in that he responded to this question with exactly the same reply as his first one.

God was probably disappointed with the response of Elijah, who seemed to be wallowing in self-pity rather than living in dependence and faith in God. God told Elijah that he was wrong about being the only prophet left – God had reserved 7,000 prophets in Israel.

Finally, it seemed that as God regarded Elijah as 'unfit for purpose', He instituted a change 'at the top' – Elijah's role would soon be taken over by his deputy, Elisha. This failure of God to change Elijah's attitude was not due to God being a poor counsellor, but it was due to the failure of Elijah to respond positively to God's wise counselling, coupled with the manifestation of His power and glory.

Sometime later Elijah and Elisha were *'walking along and talking together, suddenly a chariot of fire and horses of fire appeared and separated the two of them, and Elijah went up to heaven in a whirlwind. Elisha saw this and cried out, "My father! My father! The chariots and horsemen of Israel!" And Elisha saw him no more'* (2 Kings 2:11-12). The film 'Chariots of Fire' was based on this Biblical verse about a runner, called Harold Abrahams, who came to fame in the 1920s.

As it turns out, Elijah should not have worried about the prospect of being killed because instead of dying he was taken up to heaven in 'a chariot of fire', only to reappear 900 years later on the Mountain of Transfiguration. *'After six days Jesus took Peter, James and John with him and led them up a high mountain, where they were all alone. There he was transfigured before them. His clothes became dazzling white, whiter than anyone in the world could bleach them. And there appeared before them Elijah and Moses, who were talking with Jesus'* (Mark 9:2-4).

It would seem that after Elijah's exposure of the prophets of the false god, Baal, he suffered from what is currently known as 'bipolar disorder', characterised by extreme mood swings: these can range from extreme highs (mania) to extreme lows (depression).

I understand that the current counselling process in the NHS for clinical depression is Cognitive Behavioural Therapy, which may have some beneficial effect but I suspect there are limits to its effectiveness because it is not specifically aimed at healing the person's spirit, where the problem mainly lies. The term 'depression of spirit' is used in 2 Corinthians 2:4 (Weymouth New Testament). Clinical depression is described as 'being persistently sad for weeks or months'. It involves a feeling of hopelessness, unhappiness, low self-esteem and losing interest in things normally enjoyed. Physical symptoms include a constant feeling of being tired, sleeping badly and lack of appetite, as apparently experienced by Elijah.

Depression is described as a state of mind, in which one feels dejected or suffering from morbidly excessive melancholy. When I occasionally counselled suicidal clients, unintentionally they seemed to wallow in self-pity, placing the blame for their horrible predicament on others, rather than take any responsibility. This seems to have been the experience of Job, who stated (Job 30:16, New Living Translation), *'And now my life seeps away. Depression haunts my days.'* At times David was also depressed, saying (Psalm 143:7, New Living Translation), *'Come quickly, Lord, and answer me, for my depression deepens. Don't turn away from me, or I will die.'* Although David was caught in fear, he counteracted this fear by remembering God's work and reaching out to Him in faith.

At a crucial point in his ministry, Elijah failed an important test. How people respond to severe testing at significant times in their lives can have life-changing effects. This is illustrated in the contrasting responses to severe trials in the lives of Judas and Peter. After Judas betrayed Jesus he deeply regretted his actions and hung himself. It might have been possible for him to repent and ask the Lord's forgiveness: after all, Jesus had asked the Father to forgive those who crucified Him, as they did not know what they were doing.

Turning to Peter's experience, after denying knowing Jesus, he wept bitterly, revealing extreme remorse for disowning His Master, in the latter's time of need. In John chapter 21:15-19 it is recorded how after Jesus' resurrection, He led Peter through a counselling experience that would remove the cloud of his denial. In this passage in John's gospel, as Peter had disowned Jesus three times, three times Jesus asked Peter if he loved Him: after three affirmative answers, Jesus reinstated Peter as a leader.

God uses our tragic situations through which to attract our attention. For instance, Psalm 107:10-14 reveals one of God's strategies in drawing prisoners to faith: *'Some sat in darkness and deepest gloom, prisoners suffering in iron chains, for they had rebelled against the words of God and despised the counsel of the Most High. So he subjected them to bitter labour; they stumbled, and there was no-one to help. Then they cried to the Lord in their trouble, and he saved them from their distress. He brought them out of darkness and the deepest gloom and broke away their chains.'* Under normal circumstances many ignore God, regarding Him as superfluous to their needs. However, in some, when trouble comes this intransigent attitude seems to mellow.

The prisoners in Psalm 107 in the above paragraph were in deepest gloom or depression. Currently, in Britain, of the four million prisoners released each year, twenty-three per cent have suffered from major depressive disorders. Due to resource shortages, many go without adequate treatment while in prison. Sometimes, they return to society in a worse state than when they were first sentenced. For a few prisoners, Psalm 107:12 is relevant today: *'there was no one to help.'* The good news in Psalm 107 was that the prisoners responded to this trial in the way God wanted by crying to the Lord, who saved them from their despair and depression.

Care and empathy are required when counselling those suffering from depression. As Christians, we recognise that most depression originates from Satan. Judging from the significant increase in depression during the pandemic, it appears that Satan has been quite effective in this method of spiritual attack in seeking to control people's minds. In view of this, we should follow Paul's advice to resist the devil through self-control, one of the 'fruits of the Spirit'. 1 Peter 5:8-9: *'Be self-controlled and alert. Your enemy the devil prowls around like a roaring lion looking for someone to devour. Resist him, standing firm in the faith.'*

14.
Weaned From the World's Priorities

'My heart is not proud, O Lord, my eyes are not haughty; I do not concern myself with great matters or things too wonderful for me. But I have stilled and quietened my soul; like a weaned child with its mother, like a weaned child is my soul within me' (Psalm 131:1-2). King David warns about the danger of becoming haughty and proud. Whilst most kings would be proud of their position, David advocated humility, being content that God was in control of his life.

David used an interesting allegory – a weaned child – to describe his 'stilled and quietened soul'. Like a baby weaned from his mother's milk, the baby accepts the 'new normal' – off mum's milk and onto solid food! Similarly, due to his faith, David found peace in his soul.

Weaning a child involves enforced disengagement from a familiar habit, the spiritual allegory being self-denial. Some kind of self-denial is evident in renewal and holy obedience. In moving away from the familiar this involves thwarting our natural wishes and tastes for the things of the world. *'Do not love the world or anything in the world. If anyone loves the world, the love of the Father is not in him. For everything in the world – the cravings of sinful man, the lust of his eyes and the boasting of what he has and does – comes not from the Father but from the world. The world and its desires pass away, but the man who does the will of God lives for ever.'* (1 John 2:15-17).

The three areas of temptation in the above passage (marked below in italics) were the same areas of temptation used by Satan to tempt Eve (Genesis 3:6 – marked below with *) and by Satan to tempt Jesus in the desert (Matthew 4:1-11 – marked below with +):

Cravings of sinful man – meaning 'gratifying physical desires'.

* Eve – tempted by the fruit from the Tree of Life.

+ Lord – offered bread by Satan to meet the physical need of hunger, after fasting for forty days and nights. Satan was seeking to raise a doubt in the mind of Jesus: would God the Father provide the food He desperately needed?

Lust of the eyes – meaning 'craving for materialism'.

* Eve – fruit she was offered was 'pleasing to the eye'.

+ Lord – Satan was trying to tempt Jesus on the grounds of His possible emotional need for security, planting doubt as to whether God would protect Him if He threw Himself off the highest point on the temple?

This temptation reveals Satan's selective use of scripture, as he ends with these words (Matthew 4:6): *'so that you will not strike your foot against a stone.'* The temptation is a direct quote from Psalm 91:11-12 but Satan, no doubt deliberately, ends his scripture quotation at verse 12, as the subsequent verse is a judgement against himself: *'You* (the Lord) *will tread upon the lion and the cobra; you will trample the great lion and the serpent'* (referring to Satan).

Boasting of what he has and does – meaning 'preoccupation with status and importance'.

* Eve – tempted to doubt God's Word with the offer of wisdom and possibility of become like God – quite a prospect!

+ Lord – the purpose of the temptation was to short circuit God's plan of Salvation, avoiding crucifixion by bowing down to Satan, having been offered by the latter all the kingdoms of the world. Satan was 'playing' on the possibility of Jesus being tempted by a desire for power and achieving this with the minimum of effort.

Recently, when I was experiencing quite severe pain following an operation, I was reminded of James 1:2-4. In this passage James advised taking a positive attitude when facing trials: *'Consider it pure joy, my brothers, whenever you face trials of many kinds, because you know that the testing of your faith develops perseverance. Perseverance must finish its work so that you may be mature and complete, not lacking anything.'* To us the suggestion of becoming full of joy because of trials is difficult to accept. However, the reason James teaches this positive attitude is so that we can learn perseverance, while seeking God's long-term purposes in our lives. Children normally seek short-term solutions as they desire instant gratification, whereas adults, particularly mature Christians, should concentrate on spiritual growth, which involves an element of discipline.

Hebrews 12:5-6: *'My son, do not make light of the Lord's discipline, and do not lose heart when he rebukes you, because the Lord disciplines those he loves, and he punishes everyone he accepts as a son.'* A father reveals his love to his son when he seeks to prevent the son from doing what will harm him; this involves training, discipline and sometimes punishment. When aware of the father's discipline, the son's appropriate response should be to ask his father what he is wanting to teach him.

Returning to my post-operation experience (paragraph 5 above), I asked the Lord what He was trying to teach me and sensed that He wanted me to be 'weaned from the world's priorities'. At the time my short-term (rather worldly) priority was to be free from pain. While there is nothing wrong in desiring to be free of pain, it should not necessarily be our over-riding concern when suffering. We should also try to discern what God is trying to teach us, as He sometimes uses pain as a megaphone through which to attract our attention.

God understands that His calling on our lives will result in a clash with most of the world's priorities, so part of the Holy Spirit's ministry is to train us to look in the right direction for guidance and strength. *'Let us fix our eyes on Jesus, the author and perfecter of our faith'* (Hebrews 12:2). Our fixed gaze will indicate 'our direction of travel'. To live effectively, rather than being trapped in the world's priorities, we need to concentrate on looking to Jesus. Matthew 14:22-33 describes Christ walking on the water. When Peter saw Christ walking on the water, Peter was also able to walk on water, providing he kept his gaze on Christ. When his attention was averted to the waves on the water, he was afraid and began to sink until Christ reached out and caught him. This is an illustration of the importance of fixing our eyes in faith upon Jesus and not on the things of the world.

15.
The Importance of Marriage

When I joined the Probation Service in 1969, in addition to supervising offenders, we had various additional tasks, including settling neighbour's disputes and marriage guidance. At the time the Probation Service had more marriage guidance cases than the Marriage Guidance Service.

I felt that one of the key problematic areas behind marital disharmony was poor communication between husbands and wives. In addition, those who were married while young and immature were potentially more likely to separate, as were those who failed to acknowledge the importance of long-term commitment to each other. Many would 'walk away' from the marriage in order to avoid conflict, rather than staying and trying to deal with difficulties in the marital relationship. Most of the counselling was aimed at improving communication between the couple and addressing stressful issues, as perceived by each side. One of the areas of joy – as well as potential stress – was the arrival of children.

The Bible provides useful marriage guidance for Christians, as well as for those without a faith: God, Our Maker, knows what is best for all of us and what works and what does not work. In a discussion about divorce, Jesus explained (Mark 10:6-9), *'But at the beginning of creation*

God "made them male and female". For this reason a man will leave his father and mother and be united to his wife, and the two will become one flesh. So they are no longer two, but one. Therefore what God has joined together, let man not separate.' God wants married people to regard the marriage as permanent and not consider divorce an option for solving problems or a way out of a relationship that seems dead.

Jesus spoke against divorce (Matthew 5:32): *'But I tell you that anyone who divorces his wife, except for marital unfaithfulness, causes her to commit adultery, and anyone who marries a woman so divorced commits adultery.'* Again, Jesus is advocating the permanence of marriage, saying that divorce is only permissible on the grounds of unfaithfulness. It would appear that He is not advocating that divorce should happen automatically when a spouse commits adultery, but when an unrepentant spouse deliberately continues to lead a sexually immoral life-style.

Sir Paul Coleridge, Founder and Chairman of the Marriage Foundation, in speaking about the reasons for children's mental health problems, said, 'Many causes are cited ... but we seem to insist on turning a blind eye to the greatest underlying reason; family instability and breakdown. Unless and until we, as a mature society grasp this nettle, we will not address the main cause and will never get on top of the epidemic.'

There was a major report, funded by the Department of Health and published by the Office for National Statistics, which studied 8,000 children aged between five and sixteen years in 2004. Following are the report's findings, published in the Daily Mail on 21.10.08: 'Children from broken families are nearly five times more likely to suffer damaging mental troubles than those whose parents stay together, Government research has found. It also showed that two parents are much better than one if children are to avoid slipping into emotional distress and anti-social behaviour. The findings say that children's family backgrounds are as important – if not more so – than whether their home is poor, workless, has bad health, or has no one with any educational qualifications.'

The findings in the above paragraph mention that 'two parents are much better than one.' Therefore, some might conclude that the current 3.2 million cohabiting opposite sex couples in the UK would be able to rear their children as well as married couples. However, this idea is not supported by research. According to Benson. H., 'Annual Family Breakdown in the UK,' Marriage Foundation, March 2017, 'Although unmarried parents make up just twenty per cent of all couples with children in the UK, they account for fifty-one per cent of annual breakdowns.'

A number of great nations have imploded due to a decline in moral and spiritual values in the family, which is the basic unit and driving force within society. This was the experience of great powers, such as Greece, Persia, Babylon and Rome. We need to learn from the lessons of our forebears.

16.
Discipline in Child-Rearing

Instructions on child-rearing in the Bible sometimes conflict with current concepts on child-rearing in society. For instance, many believe in the innocence of youth, which is a notion that refers to children's simplicity, limited knowledge and purity, not yet spoiled by mundane affairs. Whereas the Bible takes the view that we are all sinful from birth. Psalm 51:5: *'Surely I have been a sinner from birth, sinful from the time my mother conceived me.'* It is most likely that the main reason the psalmist, David, wrote this was because he understood the corruption of human nature.

While reasoning with a child is usually sufficient to ensure control, there are occasions when reasoning fails to bring the child under control. In these situations, it is worth considering a smack. The child finds comfort in knowing the 'end game'. I very rarely smacked my three children and only did so after warning them, when they were persistently and deliberately disobedient. In these situations, I found that smacking provided a swift end to a dispute. When smacking a child, it is important not to do this when in a temper, as using excessive force is illegal in the UK.

It is unlawful for a parent or carer to smack their child, except where this amounts to 'reasonable punishment'. Whether or not a 'smack' amounts to reasonable punishment will depend on the circumstances of each case, taking into consideration factors like the age of the child and the nature of the smack. Proverbs 13:24: *'He who spares the rod hates his son, but he who loves him is careful to discipline him.'* The discipline of children prepares them for adult life. If children do not receive appropriate discipline, they may fail to develop a clear understanding between right and wrong.

There is a vivid example in the Old Testament about the Lord's expectation that children respect and obey their parents. Eli, who was a judge and priest in Israel had two sons, who were also priests but took advantage of their position to satisfy their lust for power, possessions and control. Eli miserably failed to control his sons, whose actions undermined the integrity of the whole priesthood. The Lord told Eli that He would judge him *"because of the sin he* (Eli) *knew about; his sons made themselves contemptible and he failed to restrain them"* (1 Samuel 3:13). Eli had spent his life in service to God but neglected his responsibilities in his own home. The sons subsequently died in battle, which was probably God's judgement on them.

Human beings are to be respected as they are made in the image of God. Genesis 9:6: *'In the image of God has God made man.'* In reply to a question by some Pharisees, Jesus reminded them of the fifth commandment: *'Honour your father and mother'* (Matthew 15:4).

Paul wrote to Timothy about the qualities of a church leader, one of them being, *'He must manage his own family well and see that his children obey him with proper respect.* (If anyone does not know how to manage his own family, how can he take care of God's church?)' (1 Timothy 3:4-5).

We should expect this human quality from our church leaders – and also perhaps our politicians.

Jesus modelled the most appropriate attitude for acceptance into the kingdom of heaven on children (Matthew 19:13-15): *'Then little children were brought to Jesus to place his hands on them and pray for them. But the disciples rebuked those who brought them. Jesus said, "Let the little children come to me, and do not hinder them, for the kingdom of heaven belongs to such as these." When he had placed his hands on them, he went on from there.'* Children have the kind of receptive attitude needed to approach God: Jesus did not mean that heaven is only for children but that people needed a childlike trust in God to be accepted into heaven.

When I was employed as a probation officer, I wrote hundreds of pre-sentence reports for Criminal Courts on offenders and also for Family Courts in regards to the custody and access of children. Discipline and child-rearing, particularly in younger offenders, usually needed to be considered in these reports. Children feel safer when the boundaries of behaviour are clearly laid down by loving and disciplined parents. Sometimes a child exhibits difficult behaviour in order to clarify for himself the boundaries of acceptable behaviour. If there are no clear boundaries, this can unsettle a child.

Pre-sentence reports for courts assisted the judiciary in sentencing and consisted of a brief life history of the client, with an emphasis on the circumstances surrounding the offence(s) before the court. I found that many offenders had very similar backgrounds. Whilst it would be foolish to classify all offenders as having the same background, nevertheless, the similarity of features in many of the clients' family background history was striking. The following four paragraphs describe some of the more frequent features in an offender's childhood experience.

Poor child-rearing and discipline were common. The child's mother separated from her partner (the putative father) in the child's early years, resulting in the child rejecting the discipline of his mother's new partner, as the child refuses to accept him as a father figure. To exacerbate the situation, the new partner is unsure of his responsibilities and role in regards to the child, who becomes rebellious and eventually so difficult to handle that the child is placed in the care of the local authority.

Mother hardly ever visits the care home to see her child, who transfers his anti-social behaviour first towards those in authority, such as his school teachers, so is regarded as a trouble maker, and later towards the police, whom he regards as bullies. He receives numerous non-custodial sentences, none of which deter him from committing further offences, often committed while in the company of other residents from his care home. His co-defendants have become his first friends; by this stage, he has earned a reputation as a 'hard man'.

For drink and drug related offences, he is placed on another Care Order, which he quite enjoys, as by now he has become a skilful manipulator; he uses his charm on his social workers in order to acquire money from them. Eventually, he is sent from court to a Young Offenders Institution, where he plans future crimes with other like-minded offenders. The offender subsequently progresses into more serious crimes, being sentenced to increasingly lengthy custodial sentences.

The above fictitious example illustrates how unruly and poorly disciplined children can sometimes end up as serious offenders. I have used this example to emphasise the importance of providing children with a good role model as a parent, coupled with consistent and fair discipline in the home. Because God loves us, He uses discipline to teach us what is right, and consequently we must do the same for our children. *'My son, do not make light of the Lord's discipline, and do not lose heart when he rebukes you, because the Lord disciplines those he loves, and he punishes everyone he accepts as a son'* (Hebrews 12:5-6).

The key verse which summarises this chapter on 'discipline in child-rearing' is from Proverbs 22:6: *'Train up a child in the way he should go, and when he is old he will not turn from it.'*

17.
Demonic Opposition

During the Lord's ministry he was frequently casting out demons in pursuance of his stated aim expressed in 1 John 3:8: *'The reason the Son of God appeared was to destroy the devil's work.'* He taught his disciples to follow His example: *'When Jesus had called the Twelve together, he gave them power and authority to drive out all demons and to cure diseases'* (Luke 9:1). On their return, the disciples appeared to be delighted that the demons had submitted to Christ's name.

Jesus responded to his disciples' enthusiastic report with these words (Luke 10:19): *'I have given you authority to trample on snakes and scorpions and to overcome all the power of the enemy.'* Casting out demons was central to Christ's ministry. However, I sense that the Church today has tended to marginalise this ministry owing to its mystifying challenges. One reason why it is mystifying is because in our scientific age we have become heavily dependent on proven visible facts, so consideration of the unseen world of demons is largely regarded as irrelevant and possibly dangerous.

Jesus described two strongly opposing spiritual kingdoms – the Kingdom of God and Satan's kingdom. He mentioned these kingdoms when responding to claims by His opponents that He was casting out demons whilst under

Satan's influence. Jesus retorted (Matthew 12:26), *'If Satan drives out Satan, he is divided against himself. How then can his* (Satan's) *kingdom stand?'* Jesus added (Matthew 12:28), *'But if I drive out demons by the Spirit of God, then the kingdom of God has come upon you.'*

During several encounters the Lord had with demons, the opening remarks came from the demons (through the 'victim's voice'), accurately calling Jesus, the 'Son of God'. How did they know Jesus' identity, when most people around Jesus were unaware of His true nature? The reason the demons recognised Jesus was because they had previously been angels in heaven with Him. Satan and some angels became rebellious, so were thrown out of heaven, instead becoming demons on earth. Revelations 12:7: *'And there was war in heaven. Michael and his angels fought against the dragon'* (Satan), who was not strong enough. Consequently Satan, with the rebellious third of the heavenly host, was 'hurled to the earth'.

As disembodied spirits, the demons' main intention has always been to inhabit a body (preferably human), from where their aim is to stop their host becoming a Christian. If they fail in this aim, their tactics change to attempting to prevent their host effectively serving the Lord. Satan is known as a 'deceiver', so his fellow demons have become adept at manipulating people through enticement, tormenting, defiling and enslaving. On discovering areas in which we are not in control of ourselves, we need to consider whether this is either due to our fallen nature, or whether in the particular slavish area of our lives we are being controlled by an outside agent(s), who in the Bible are given various names, such as demons, evil spirits or unclean spirits.

This oppression by one or more demons is normally called demonic activity. A more serious condition is demonic possession, where the person's whole nature is taken over. Whilst a Christian can be troubled by demonic oppression, he or she cannot be demon possessed, as at the new birth of a Christian the Holy Spirit enters the person, so there is no room for demons.

There are plenty of places where demons can take up residence within us. A few examples are in our emotions, mind, addictions, and lusts. We need to be careful about getting involved in horoscopes and fortune telling, which can expose us to unwanted demonic attack. When in a weak state, or after a serious accident, we are more susceptible to these attacks. Physical ailments, such as epilepsy, can come from an evil spirit: Jesus healed several different diseases by casting out the particular demon, which was causing the disease or ailment.

This is a complicated subject. I found Derek Prince's website (www.derekprince.com) helpful in explaining and illustrating how people can be delivered from demons. Derek stresses the necessity for those seeking deliverance to come with a humble attitude and a passionate desire to be freed.

God desperately wants us to love Him. The first of the Ten Commandments sums up God's expectation and requirement of us (Exodus 20:3): *'You shall have no other gods before me.'* The second commandment is similar (Exodus 20:4): *'You shall not make for yourself an idol.'* Later in this commandment there is this surprising statement: *'I, the Lord, your God, am a jealous God, punishing the children for the sin of the fathers to the third and fourth generation of those who hate me.'* Whilst it may seem to us harsh punishing the children for their parents' sins, the reality is that it matters not what we think because God is in control and makes the rules in this world.

The second commandment about not having an idol is mainly directed towards everything to do with the occult, which involves demonically inspired supernatural beliefs and practices that are detestable to God. Therefore, it is particularly important for ourselves, our children and grandchildren that we keep ourselves free from occult practices. We do not want to open ourselves, or family members, to demonic influence.

A favourite 'residence' for demons is in sexual perversion. I suspect that a number of sex offences are demonically inspired. When employed as a probation officer, I was surprised at the statistics which showed a large percentage of sex offenders had themselves been abused in childhood, sometimes by their fathers, thus fulfilling the judgement stated for ignoring the Second Commandment, when the sins of the fathers result in the punishment of their children and grandchildren. Hence the importance of 'curing' sex offenders, as is beneficial both for the offender, as well as hopefully severing the potential for a familial pattern of offending.

Whilst we should avoid 'perceiving' demons in everything, nevertheless, on becoming aware of an area in one's life which is getting control, one of the causes could be demonic oppression, so it is possibly worth seeking appropriate Christian advice.

18.
Put On Your Listening Ears

Luke 8:16-18: *'No-one lights a lamp and hides it in a jar or puts it under a bed. Instead, he puts it on a stand, so that those who come in can see the light. For there is nothing hidden that will not be disclosed, and nothing concealed that will not be known or brought out into the open. Therefore consider carefully how you listen. Whoever has will be given more; whoever does not have, even what he thinks he has will be taken from him.'*

Christ told his disciples the above parable so that they could understand when the light of the truth about Christ illuminates us, it is our duty to pass on this light to enlighten others. This parable emphasises the importance of carefully considering how we listen to God's Word, so that we are enabled to grow spiritually. We need to be attentive to what we hear, retain a prayerful state of mind and be careful to understand what we sense through meditation, by applying God's Word to our lives.

The last sentence of the above parable opens up an interesting principle. 'Whoever has will be given more; whoever does not have, even what he thinks he has will be taken from him.' This refers to the self-delusion of presuming one has understanding, when this is not the case, as the person concerned has not applied the knowledge effectively to his own conduct and life. Consequently, he will lose the slight insight which he had originally possessed. Whereas the person who takes careful note to what he hears, believing it to be true and obeying it, is in a fit state to receive more knowledge. Christ was not reproaching His disciples, but warning them to take care in regards to this principle.

In effect those who have a deep spiritual understanding will receive more wisdom, whilst those who delude themselves into thinking they have this understanding will lose the little that they have. Whilst I totally concur with this principle, many in our present day and age might regard this as unfair, believing that all should receive the same, so that no-one is a loser (in the parable in the above paragraph, the little the 'loser' had was taken away).

One of my grandsons recently told me that his school sports day did not include any competitive sports so that no-one would lose in the races. I cannot understand how it can be helpful to try to protect children from the disappointment of losing in an inherently competitive society, where competitive interviews are part of the normal selection process for employment.

We need to take note of Christ's words, "carefully consider how you listen." Rather than slipping into 'sleep mode', we should train ourselves not only to meditate carefully on what is said, but also determine, where appropriate, to adopt the new doctrine of teaching into our daily conduct.

The American TV Judge Judy has coined an interesting catchphrase, "Put on your listening ears." Our Lord also had a similar catchphrase, which he used twice in Matthew's gospel and once in Mark's Gospel, *"He who has ears, let him hear!"* (Matthew 11:15). There is a deep kind of listening which results in spiritual understanding. Genuinely seeking God's will enlightens our spiritual understanding, so that Christ's teaching takes on new meaning and encouragement.

Christ used parables to explain some of the mysteries of the kingdom of heaven in order that they might be understood by some (disciples and seekers) but not others (His enemies). Quite often after Christ's discourses, the disciples asked Him privately the meaning of the parables. In giving the disciples additional explanation about the parables, Christ's intention was that they should pass this information onto others. It was through the apostles' gospels and letters that Christ's additional teaching was included, encouraging disciples to diffuse this spiritual light to others.

The illustration of this diffusion of light was described by Christ as putting a lamp on a stand so that it could be easily seen by others. If we are to be a good witness, Christ's teaching needs to be seen to be operative in our lives, so that the eyes of the hearts of many might be enlightened to see the glory of God. Living for Christ illuminates us so that we glow, revealing to others what Christ is like.

'Let your light shine before men, that they may see your good deeds and praise your Father in heaven' (Matthew 5:16). How is this 'light' first conveyed to us? Paul explains that it is through the Holy Spirit (1 Corinthians 2:10-13): *'The Spirit searches all things, even the deep things of God. For who among men knows the thoughts of a man except the man's spirit within him? In the same way no-one knows*

the thoughts of God except the Spirit of God. We have not received the spirit of the world but the Spirit who is from God, that we may understand what God has freely given us. This is what we speak, not in words taught us by human wisdom, but in words taught by the Spirit, expressing spiritual truths in spiritual words.'

When we listen carefully God reveals His heart to us. While we cannot know the things of God, the Holy Spirit, who is one with the Father and the Son can make the divine mysteries of God known to us. We can be taught by the Holy Spirit and in turn declare the truths of God in plain, simple language to others. The sanctified mind discerns the wonderful nature of God. At Pentecost the disciples were so filled with the Holy Spirit that they could not help but declare God's glories to people of different nations, in their own languages, as the Spirit gave them utterance. At Pentecost the tongues of fire that rested on each of the disciples would have shone as bright lights, pointing to 'The Way'. The effect of the Holy Spirit's power that day resulted in 3,000 people becoming believers, after having been drawn to the 'Light of the World', who is the Lord Jesus Christ.

19.
Our Relationship with the Lord Jesus Christ

A Christian's relationship with the Lord Jesus Christ is probably the most important thing in life. No amount of law-keeping, self-improvement, discipline or religious effort will give us 'righteousness' (which means 'being in a right relationship with God'). Paul explains that righteousness comes through knowing God. He explains this in Philippians 3:8-11: *'I consider everything a loss compared to the surpassing greatness of knowing Christ Jesus my Lord, for whose sake I have lost all things. I consider them rubbish, that I may gain Christ and be found in him, not having a righteousness of my own, that comes from the law, but that which is through faith in Christ – the righteousness that comes from God and is by faith. I want to know Christ and the power of his resurrection and the fellowship of sharing in his sufferings, becoming like him in his death, and so, somehow, to attain to the resurrection from the dead.'*

Paul wrote about gaining Christ and being found in him. We need to be careful not to rely too much on our attempts at 'forcing this relationship', which would then rely on our actions. Paul writes about being 'found (of God) in him' – this action is through God's grace. We need to possess Christ in all our faculties. Our head and heart should possess Christ's passions and desires and these in turn should guide us into a nobler life as we follow Christ, who lives in Christians. We gradually become conformed to Christ's likeness, through the sanctifying work of the Holy Spirit.

A fundamental element of our relationship with Christ is the knowledge and experience of having a personal acquaintance with Him. This is not a mere theoretical or intellectual knowledge but one for which Paul 'lost all things', so it is costly and involves 'sharing in his sufferings'. It needs to be experienced to be fully understood, in the same way as a man only knows the bliss of parental or wedded love by personally experiencing it.

There are plenty of statements about Christ's life and teaching, as well as various names describing His wonderful personality and ministry; we need to meditate on these, under the guidance of the Holy Spirit, who inspires and enlightens us through God's Word. This meditation should encourage us to earnestly seek personal experience of the 'Living Lord'.

When 'we touch base' with the Holy Spirit, He stimulates our spirits to respond in love, compassion and an inner understanding of Christ. Consequently, we hunger for more experience of Christ, so that, like deer seeking the refreshment of water, we become eager to seek refreshment from Christ, who is the 'Living Water'.

Psalm 42: 1-2: *'As the deer pants for streams of water, so my soul pants for you, O God. My soul thirsts for God, for the living God. When can I go and meet with God?'* Deer pant and thirst for water. In a similar way we 'thirst' after God. Thirst is a perpetual feeling, as is our continual longing after God. This psalmist felt separated from God and would not rest until he had restored his relationship with Him.

The psalmist revealed a pious heart with an intensity to meet with God. However, he felt 'cut off' from God as in both verses 5 and 11 of Psalm 42 he wrote the same words: *'Why are you downcast, O my soul? Why so disturbed within me?'* The psalmist was probably discouraged because he and his nation had been exiled to a place far from Jerusalem, so could not worship in the temple.

There can be a variety of reasons why we may feel 'distant from God', the most common being due to unconfessed sin. It is encouraging to remember what has been termed 'the great exchange', which happens when we are 'born again' – in repentance we hand God our sins and in return receive God's forgiveness and righteousness. God is holy and will not tolerate sin in His presence, so refuses to listen to our requests if we approach Him with unconfessed sin in our hearts. *'If I had cherished sin in my heart, the Lord would not have listened'* (Psalm 66:18).

God is attuned and responsive to our desires. If we really want to contact Him, we need to accept in faith that He will manifest Himself in accordance to His Word (James 4:8): *'Come near to God and he will come near to you.'* God graciously waits to respond to our calling and seeking Him, like the father waiting for the appearance of his prodigal son. On seeing his son returning, the father ran out to hug and welcome him. Although God is always eager to welcome us into His presence, He graciously waits for us to 'make the first move'. What changed everything for the prodigal son was his decision, while in a desperate situation, to return to his father.

We are often shy about letting others know us completely but God already knows all about us, so it is useless to 'hide' our inner selves from Him. David wrote in Palm 139: 1-4 about God being all-seeing, all-knowing, all powerful and present everywhere and how He utilises these attributes to develop a personal knowledge for us: *'O Lord, you have searched me and you know me. You know when I sit and when I rise; you perceive my thoughts from afar. You discern my going out and my lying down; you are familiar with all my ways. Before a word is on my tongue you know it completely, O Lord.'* In the first verse of this psalm, David told God, 'You know me' – God has taken the trouble to know us so we need to get to know Him.

'Now this is eternal life; that they may know you, the only true God, and Jesus Christ, whom you have sent' (John 17:3). This statement was part of Christ's prayer to His Father shortly before His crucifixion. In this verse Christ stated that eternal life is knowing God the Father, through Christ, who is the exact representation of God the Father. Eternal life involves entering into a personal relationship with God through the Lord Jesus Christ.

20.
Making Our Calling and Election Sure

For this chapter it may be helpful to keep your Bible open at 1 and 2 Peter. These short letters were written by Peter to the churches in Asia Minor (north-west Turkey). At the time the Christians in that area were suffering persecution, so Peter's aim was to encourage them to endure persecution, mainly by reminding them of their great salvation. The meaning of salvation is the transformation of a person's nature and relationship with God as a result of repentance and faith in the sacrificial death of the Lord Jesus Christ. It is interesting that the UK's National Anthem, since the beginning of the nineteenth century ('God save our gracious Queen'), involves requesting from God the salvation of the reigning monarch.

It is quite probable that a number of the Christians who originally received these two letters came to salvation as a result of Peter's first sermon at Pentecost. It is therefore fitting that in his opening address to them, he summarises the main function of each member of the Trinity in the process of salvation. He describes his readers as 'God's elect', *'who have been chosen according to the foreknowledge of God the Father, through the sanctifying work of the Spirit, for obedience to Jesus Christ and sprinkling by his blood'* (1 Peter 1:2).

The above verse explains the function of God the Father as foreknowing those whom He chose for salvation. In Ephesians 1:4, Paul expands on this statement, *'For he* (the Father) *chose us in him* (Christ) *before the creation of the world.'* This is an amazing and wonderful truth. However, some might regard it as unfair in that God chooses some and not others. In fact, this is not unfair because God is God and can do what He wants in His universe. In any case, God sees our choice of salvation in advance of the time, which does not necessarily mean He influences that choice. 1 Timothy 2:3-4: *'God our Saviour, who wants all men to be saved and to come to a knowledge of the truth.'* God wants all to be saved, but as a Realist, knows this will not happen because He has allowed each person the option to choose death and separation from God in place of His offer of eternal salvation with Christ.

Moving on to the function of the Holy Spirit (1 Peter 1:2) – 'through the sanctifying work of the Spirit.' The Holy Spirit sets us apart for holy service, in conformity with the nature of Christ. The purpose of the functions of both the Father and the Son is 'for obedience to Jesus Christ and sprinkling by his blood.' Christ expects us to obey Him so directed His disciples to this effect: *'If anyone loves me, he will obey my teaching'* (John 14:23). It is necessary that we are sprinkled by Christ's blood because *'without the shedding of blood there is no forgiveness'* (Hebrews 9:22).

2 Peter 1:5-9 describes the intended development of Christian character. This passage is about faith which is more than just belief in certain facts about God. Faith should result in the growth of Christian character and moral discipline, through the seven qualities (listed in 2 Peter 1:5-

9) that come out of faith. It is well worth developing these qualities in order to make our 'calling and election sure' (2 Peter 1:10). The term 'calling' here does not refer to a calling to a position but an individual's calling to salvation. This encouragement for growth in Christian character and the practice of moral discipline challenges Christians to avoid complacency. 2 Peter 1:10 is also a reminder of God's practice of making His promises conditional on our obedience to His Word. In this case, God has saved us but in return we must love and obey Him.

The spiritual growth and maturity of the Christians in Asia Minor enabled them to face persecution from external forces. Their faith was also being tested through internal 'opposition' forces within the churches. These internal pressures came from false teachers, who *secretly introduce destructive heresies, even denying the sovereign Lord'* (2 Peter 2:1). The false teachers were suggesting that self-control and spiritual discipline were not required. However, Peter countered this argument by stimulating the Christians to seek to develop spiritual qualities, including self-control, in order to be 'eager to make their calling and election sure'. We are saved to follow Christ and through our faith in Him, serve others.

Another way Peter suggested combating false teachers was with the truth of Scripture. *'Above all, you must understand that no prophecy of Scripture came about by the prophet's own interpretation. For prophecy never had its origin in the will of man, but men spoke from God as they were carried along by the Holy Spirit'* (2 Peter 1:20). This statement makes it clear that God the Father, through the Holy Spirit, inspires prophets to write the Scriptures: this leaves no room for prophets to add a few thoughts of their own. The truth and authenticity of Scripture is confirmed in 2 Timothy 3:16: *'All Scripture is God-breathed'* or, as the King James Bible states, 'All scripture is by inspiration of God.' The term 'prophet' in this context does not only refer to the Old Testament prophets but also to those people of God in the Old and New Testament (like Peter) who, while inspired by the Holy Spirit, disclosed to others the will and purposes of God.

Another internal threat to the faith of the Christians in Asia Minor was the 'scoffers' – plenty of them in our day and age! The scoffers were suggesting that Jesus was never going to return to Earth. *'First of all, you must understand that in the last days scoffers will come, scoffing and following their own evil desires. They will say, 'Where is this "coming" he promised? Ever since our fathers died, everything goes on as it has since the beginning of creation'* (2 Peter 3:3-4).

Peter refuted the scoffers by explaining what would happen when the Lord returns, calling His return date as 'the day of the Lord'. *'But the day of the Lord will come like a thief. The heavens will disappear with a roar; the elements will be destroyed by fire, and the earth and everything in it will be laid bare'* (2 Peter 3:10).

Whilst we should be responsible for properly looking after the good things that God has given us, including the Earth, when Scripture states that the heavens (or universe) will disappear with a roar and the Earth be completely destroyed by fire, this rather overshadows the current fears of many about climate change, the ozone layer and deforestation. God's Word on this matter should refocus concerns onto the eternal perspective, including God's plan for the Earth.

Peter makes a challenging statement near the end of his second letter (2 Peter 3:11-13): *'Since everything will be destroyed in this way, what kind of people ought you to be? You ought to live holy and godly lives as you look forward to the day of God and speed its coming. That day will bring about the destruction of the heavens by fire, and the elements will melt in the heat. But in keeping with his promise we are looking forward to a new heaven and a new earth, the home of righteousness.'*

If we seek to 'make our calling and election sure', on Judgement Day we should then qualify, with others, to spend eternity with Our Lord Jesus Christ in 'a new heaven and a new earth, the home of righteousness.'

21.
The Shrewd Manager

When I was reading Luke chapter 16 about the parable of the Shrewd Manager, at first I thought the Lord was recommending dishonest practice. In order to obtain clarification, I looked up this chapter on the website www.biblehub.com.

Jesus told this parable about a rich man (representing God) who had appointed a manager over His affairs. Christ's teaching was specifically designed for his audience, which were his disciples and some Pharisees.

The rich man accused the manager of wasting his master's possessions so asked for an explanation. After the meeting with his master the manager, who knew he would be dismissed, called in a number of his master's debtors, telling them to quickly settle their accounts by paying much less for the commodities than they were originally charged.

Jesus continues the parable (Luke 16:8-13): *'The master commended the dishonest manager because he had acted shrewdly. For the people of this world are more shrewd in dealing with their own kind than are the people of the light. I tell you, use worldly wealth to gain friends for yourselves, so that when it is gone, you will be welcomed into eternal dwellings. Whoever can be trusted with very little can also be trusted with much, and whoever is dishonest with very little will also be dishonest with much.*

So if you have not been trustworthy in handling worldly wealth, who will trust you with true riches? And if you have not been trustworthy with someone else's property, who will give you property of your own? No servant can serve two masters. Either he will hate the one and love the other, or he will be devoted to the one and despise the other. You cannot serve both God and Money.'

Through this parable, Jesus was seeking to encourage His believers to behave wisely in what is committed to their trust, ensuring God's gifts and talents are used to His glory: the more we are given, the more that is expected from us.

The Pharisees were known to be rich and presumably shrewd with their money. No doubt they would have been pleased at the rather shrewd and underhand way the manager in the parable had operated towards his master's debtors – possibly they would have taken the same action in that situation! However, their elation was short-lived when Jesus revealed the parable's 'sting in the tail' was directed against them. (Luke 16:14-15): *'The Pharisees, who loved money, heard all this and were sneering at Jesus. He said to them, "You are the ones who justify yourselves in the eyes of men, but God knows your hearts. What is highly valued among men is detestable in God's sight."'*

By now the Pharisees realised that Christ was criticizing their obstinacy to everything that He taught. The shrewd manager's actions were an illustration of their selfish desires to secure and improve their financial interests.

In extending this teaching to our use of money, a good test in our lives of the lordship of Christ is whether our resources are exclusively for ourselves, or whether they are also used for the good of others. It is important to use our goods to foster faith and obedience. Heaven's riches are far more important than earthly wealth.

To summarise this parable, Christ was not seeking to justify dishonesty or fraud but rather to point out the careful ways of worldly men. He wanted the disciples to learn wisdom from worldly men as this would enable the disciples to better pursue their objectives. Christians need to make wise use of financial opportunities, not to earn heaven, but so that heaven ("eternal dwellings") will be a welcome experience for those we seek to help. We need to unselfishly help others by using our earthly investments and spiritual resources for heavenly benefit.

'What is highly valued among men is detestable in God's sight' (Luke 16:15). This statement is probably a reference to what Christ had just taught: *'You cannot serve both God and Money'* (Luke 16:13). The word 'serve' is significant, because we serve what we love: money in itself is not wrong but serving, or loving, money is wrong – it is placing priority on money before God.

What is 'highly valued' by humanity needs to be tested against God's priorities and truths. I advocate God's truths because I believe in Jesus' words, which are the title of this book, *'The Truth will set you Free'* (John 8:32). The 'truth', as seen by the world, is sometimes 'detestable' to God, being in opposition to His truth. In this book I have considered some of the world's questionable concepts and beliefs, such as evolution, abortion and horoscopes by counterbalancing these with God's truths as expressed in the Bible. I have also outlined God's doctrines in regards to fundamental elements of life, like creation, marriage, child-rearing and demonic opposition. As you study the Bible, I hope and pray that you find it a fascinating, challenging, life-changing Book, inspired by the Holy Spirit.

Peter Denison has written two books on prison ministry, published by Olympia Publishers:-

Freedom for Prisoners – ISBN: 978-1-80074-245-1
Freedom in Christ – ISBN: 978-1-80074-378-6

Printed in Great Britain
by Amazon

35192893R00061